Sexy Angels
Sexy Photo Books of Seductive Girls

Erotic Photography of Sexy Girls

By Sexy Angel

Published by:
Sexy Angel

ISBN-13: 978-1508473138
ISBN-10: 1508473137

Fabric

www.ingramcontent.com/pod-product-compliance
Lightning Source LLC
Chambersburg PA
CBHW050409180526
45159CB00005B/2210
* 9 7 8 1 5 0 8 4 7 3 1 3 8 *